Contents

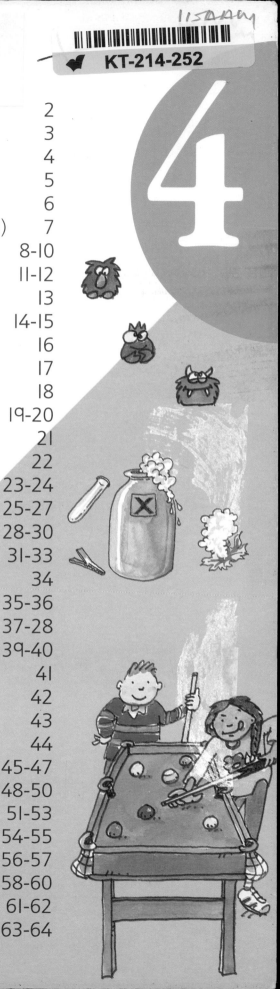

How to use this book

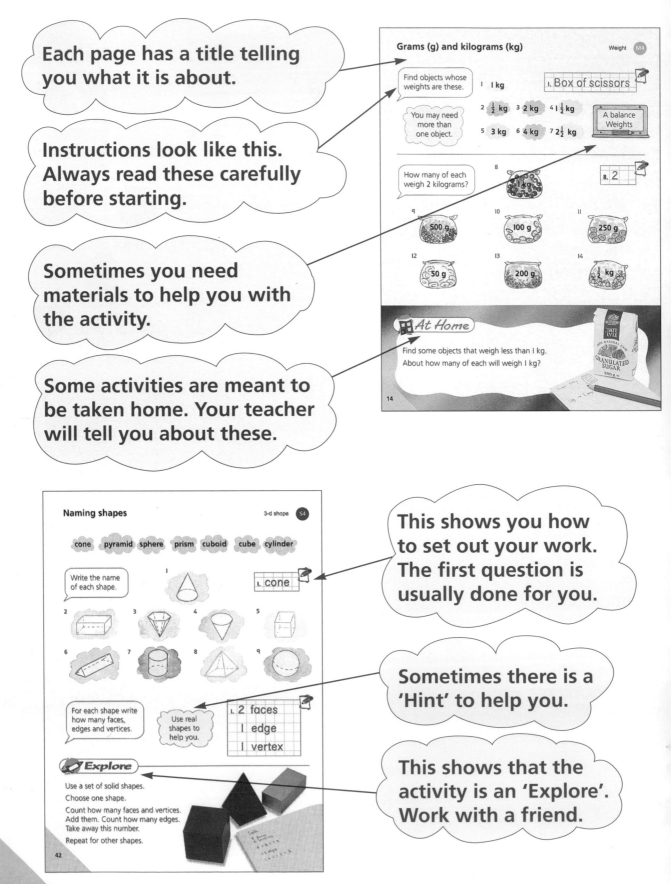

Each page has a title telling you what it is about.

Instructions look like this. Always read these carefully before starting.

Sometimes you need materials to help you with the activity.

Some activities are meant to be taken home. Your teacher will tell you about these.

This shows you how to set out your work. The first question is usually done for you.

Sometimes there is a 'Hint' to help you.

This shows that the activity is an 'Explore'. Work with a friend.

Centimetres (cm)

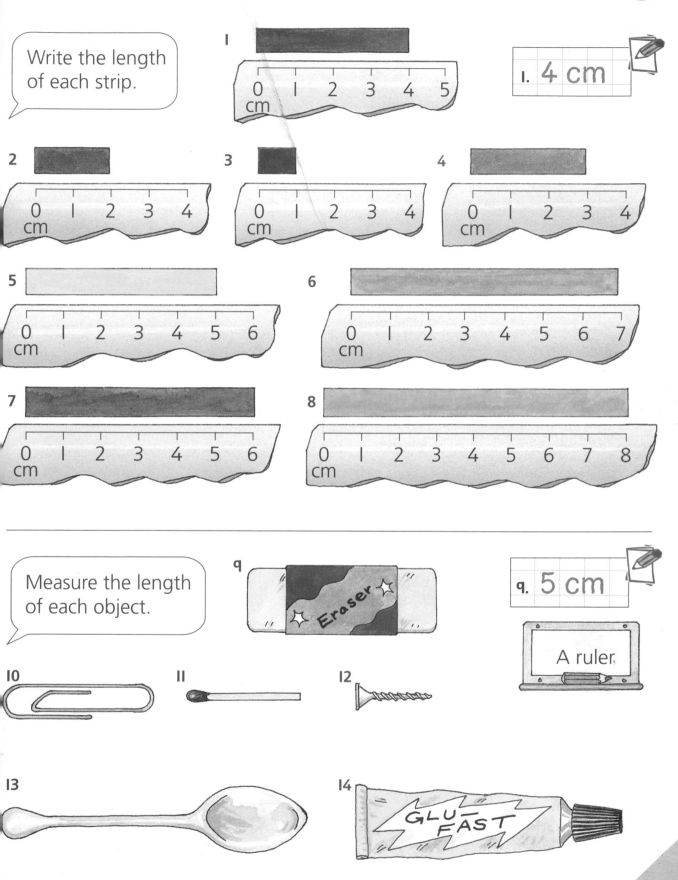

Write the length of each strip.

1. 4 cm

Measure the length of each object.

9. 5 cm

A ruler.

Centimetres (cm) and metres (m)

Write how many centimetres.

1 1 m 20 cm

1. 120 cm

2 1 m 10 cm

3 2 m

4 1 m 80 cm

5 2 m 30 cm

6 $2\frac{1}{2}$ m

7 1 m 64 cm

Write how many metres and centimetres.

8 130 cm

8. 1 m 30 cm

9 110 cm

10 170 cm

11 205 cm

12 420 cm

13 350 cm

14 300 cm

Centimetres (cm)

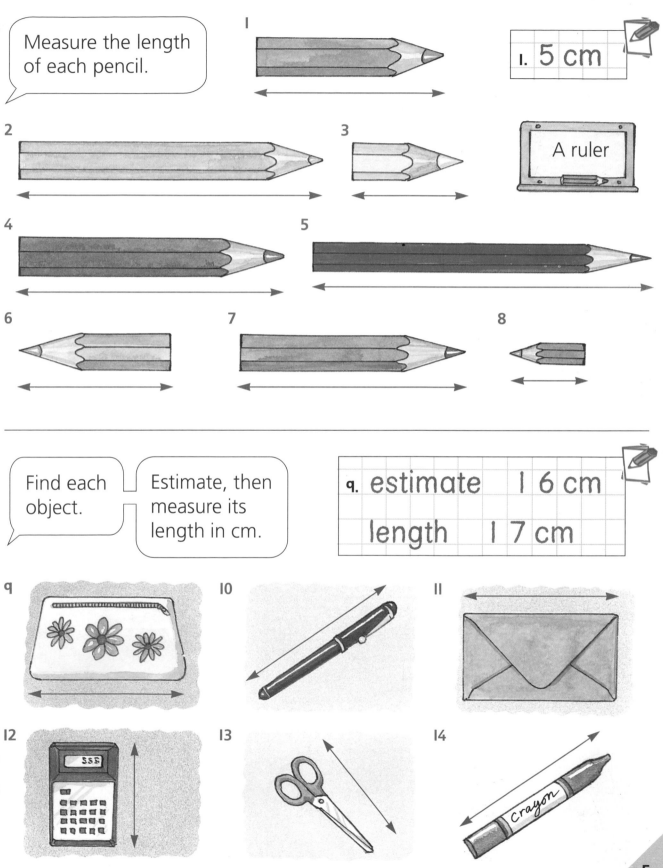

Measure the length of each pencil.

1. 5 cm

2.

3.

A ruler

4.

5.

6.

7.

8.

Find each object.

Estimate, then measure its length in cm.

9. estimate   1 6 cm

length   1 7 cm

9.

10.

11.

12.

13.

14. crayon

5

Decimetres (dm) and metres (m)

Write each length in decimetres.

1. **1 m 3 dm**

1. 13 dm

2. **1 m 5 dm**

3. **2 m 3 dm**

4. **2 m 1 dm**

5. **4 m 9 dm**

6. **3 m 7 dm**

7. **5 m**

Write each length in metres and decimetres.

8. **16 dm**

8. 1 m 6 dm

9. **19 dm**

10. **21 dm**

11. **30 dm**

12. **44 dm**

13. **15 dm**

14. **56 dm**

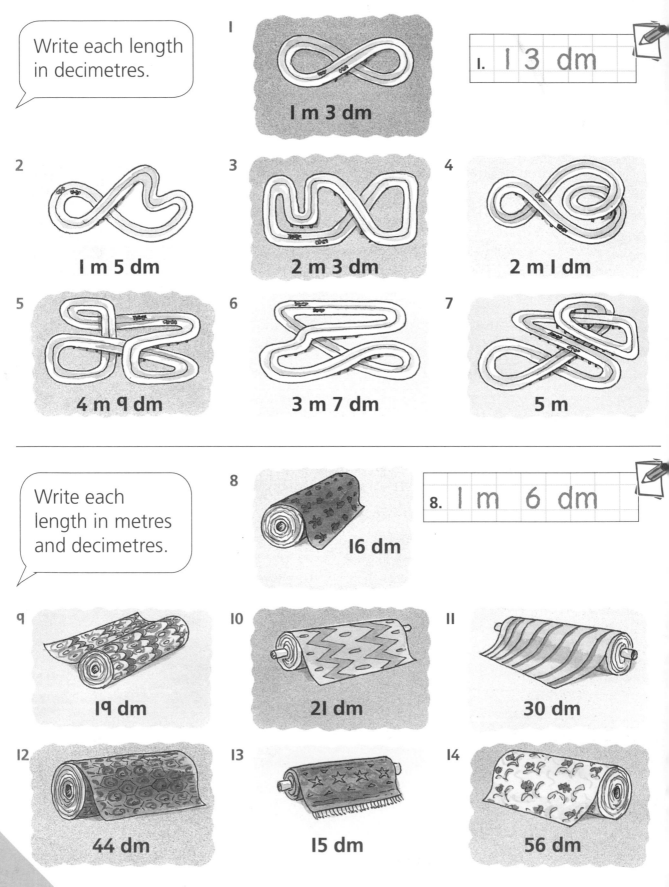

Centimetres (cm), decimetres (dm) and metres (m)

Write each length in decimetres.

1   4 m   1. 40 dm

2   2 m   3   1 m   4 $\frac{1}{2}$ m   5 $3\frac{1}{2}$ m   6   5 m

Write each length above in centimetres.

1. 400 cm

Write each length in metres.

7   200 cm   7. 2 m

8   100 cm   9   70 dm   10   1000 cm   11   5 dm   12   30 dm

Explore

Work with a partner.

Measure each other's height and reach.

Write the measurements in:

(a) cm   (b) dm   (c) m and cm.

Do the same for other body measurements: arm length, waist, ...

height   reach

The squares are square centimetres.

Write the area of each rectangle.

1. $A = 3 \times 5$
$= 15 \text{ cm}^2$

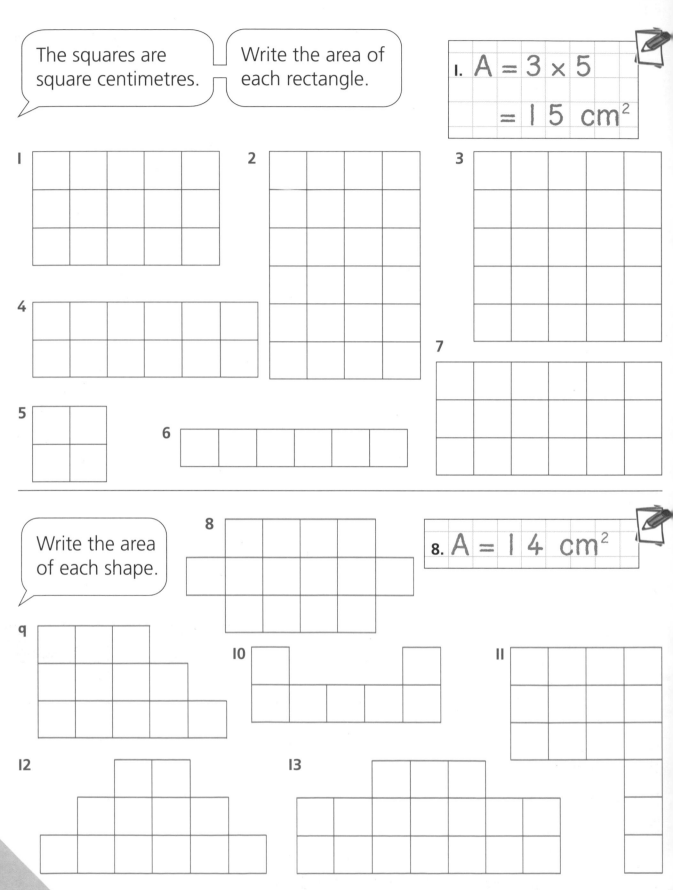

Write the area of each shape.

8. $A = 14 \text{ cm}^2$

Area

> The squares are square centimetres.

> Write the area of each shape.

I. $A = 3 \times 3$
$= 9 \ cm^2$

1

2

3

4

5

6

7

Explore

Draw 10 different rectangles on squared paper, then cut them out.

Put them in order from smallest area to largest area, by estimating.

Finally, find their areas by multiplying, writing them on the rectangles. Was your estimated order correct?

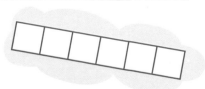

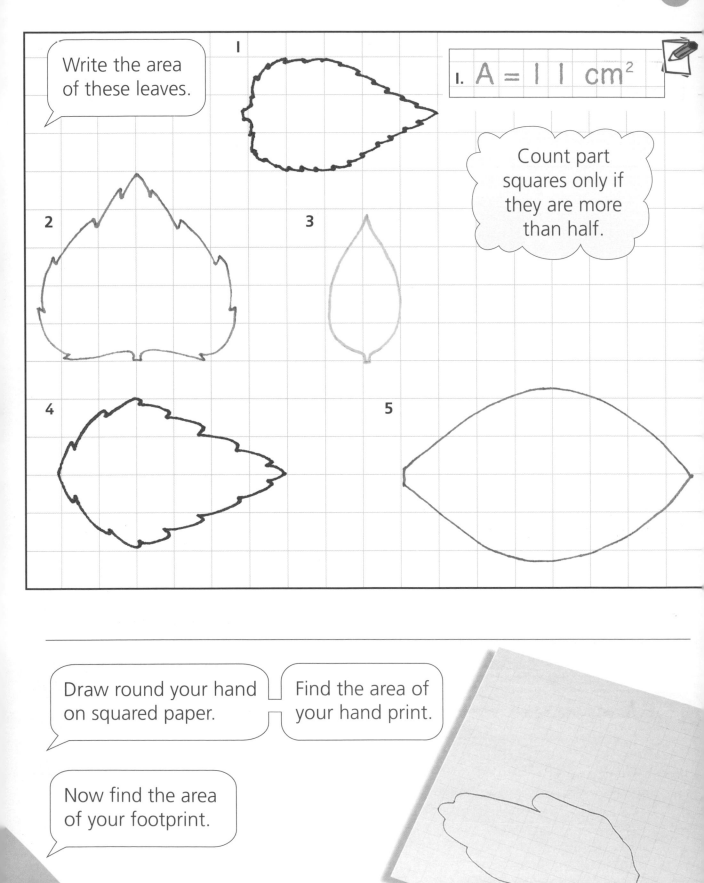

Write the area of these leaves.

1

1. A = 1 1 cm²

Count part squares only if they are more than half.

2

3

4

5

Draw round your hand on squared paper.

Find the area of your hand print.

Now find the area of your footprint.

Perimeter and area

Write the perimeter of each shape.

1.

ı. P = 8 cm

2

3

4

5

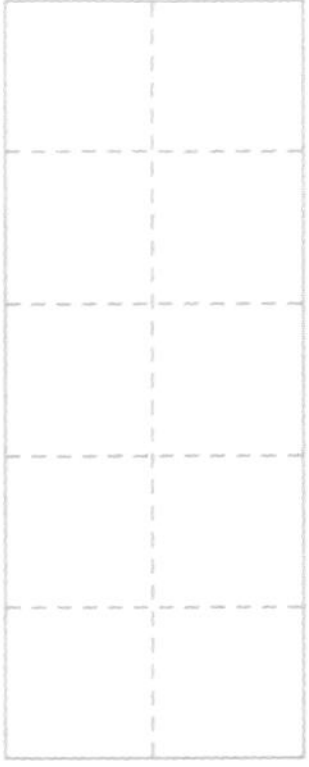

6

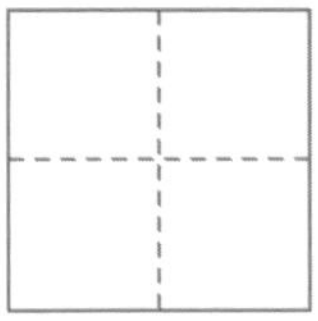

7

8

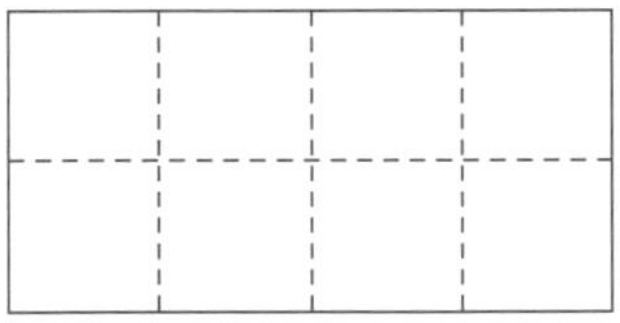

9

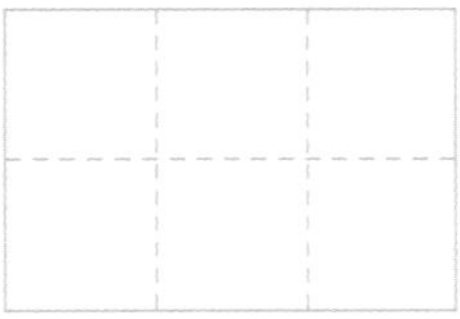

10

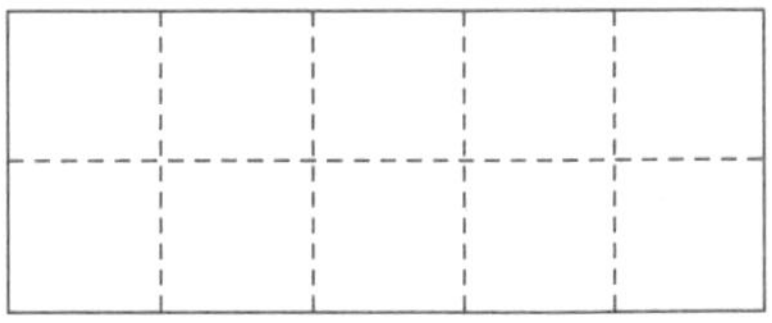

Which three shapes have the same perimeter?

Write the area of each shape.

ı. A = 3 cm²

Explore

Draw different rectangles on squared paper.

Write the perimeter and area of each.

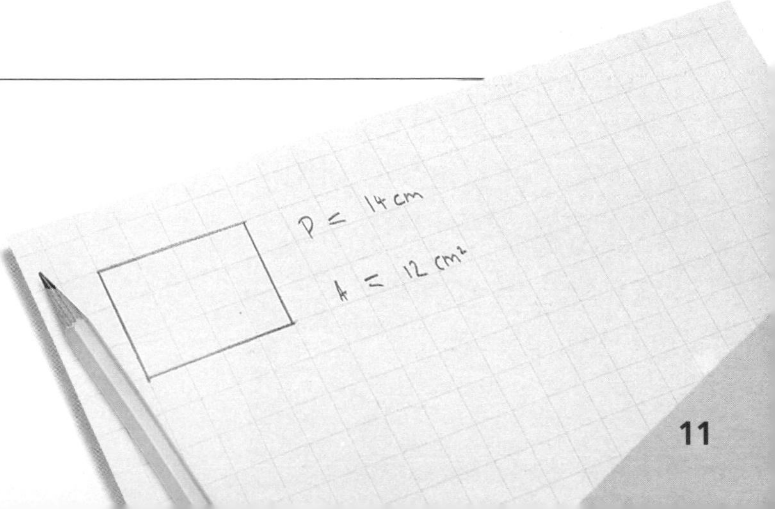

P = 14 cm

A = 12 cm²

Perimeter and area

Each tile is I dm square.

Write the perimeter and area of each blue shape.

I. P = 8 dm
   A = 3 dm²

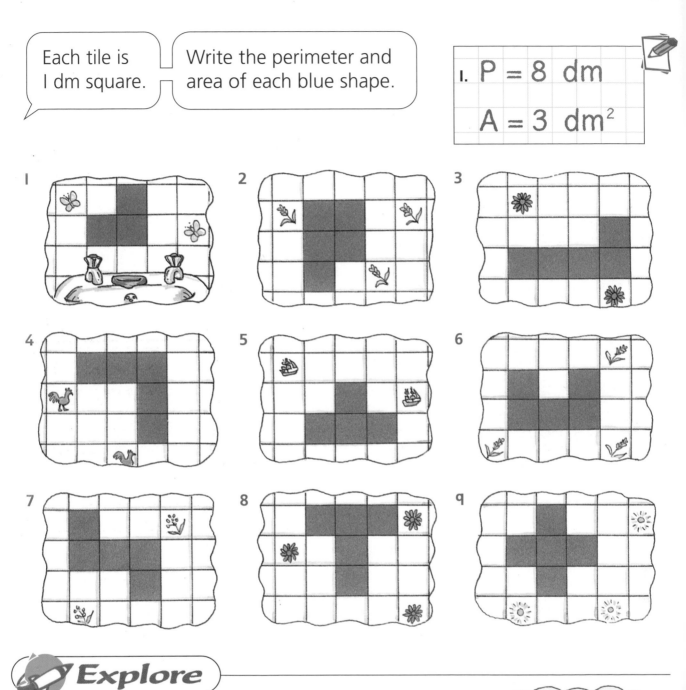

1   2   3

4   5   6

7   8   q

Explore

This shape has a perimeter of I0 cm.

Draw other shapes with a perimeter of I0 cm.

Use a set of squares to help you.

P = I0 cm

Perimeter

Measure the sides of each stamp.

Write the perimeters.

I. P = I 2 cm

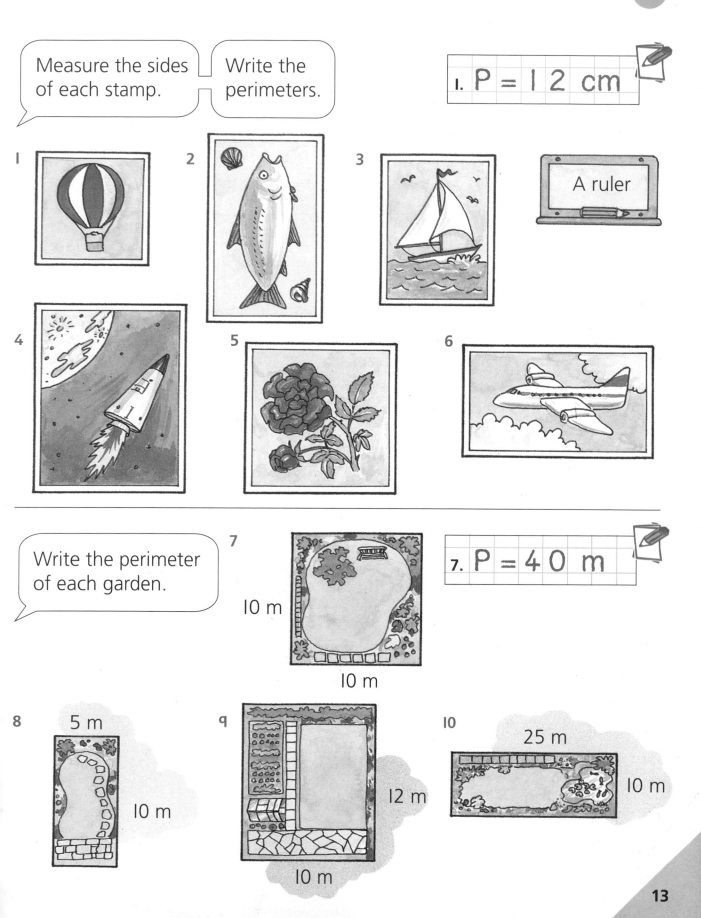

1

2

3

A ruler

4

5

6

Write the perimeter of each garden.

7

10 m

10 m

7. P = 4 0 m

8 5 m

10 m

9

12 m

10 m

10 25 m

10 m

Grams (g) and kilograms (kg)

Find objects whose weights are these.

You may need more than one object.

1 1 kg

2 $\frac{1}{2}$ kg   3 2 kg   4 1$\frac{1}{2}$ kg

5 3 kg   6 4 kg   7 2$\frac{1}{2}$ kg

1. Box of scissors

A balance
Weights

How many of each weigh 2 kilograms?

8

1 kg

8. 2

9

500 g

10

100 g

11

250 g

12

50 g

13

200 g

14

$\frac{1}{2}$ kg

At Home

Find some objects that weigh less than 1 kg.

About how many of each will weigh 1 kg?

TATE LYLE

FROM NATURAL CANE

GRANULATED SUGAR

500 g e

Sugar 500g

1 kg → 2 bags

Grams (g) and kilograms (kg)

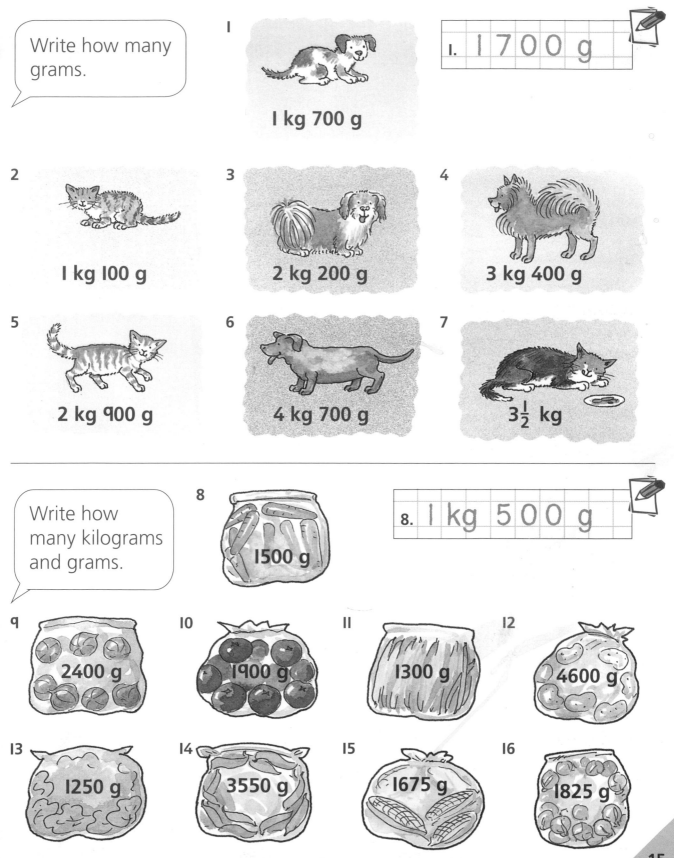

Write how many grams.

1

1 kg 700 g

1. 1 7 0 0 g

2

1 kg 100 g

3

2 kg 200 g

4

3 kg 400 g

5

2 kg 900 g

6

4 kg 700 g

7

$3\frac{1}{2}$ kg

Write how many kilograms and grams.

8

1500 g

8. 1 kg 5 0 0 g

9

2400 g

10

1900 g

11

1300 g

12

4600 g

13

1250 g

14

3550 g

15

1675 g

16

1825 g

Write how many millilitres of juice in each container.

1. 1 litre

1. 600 ml

2. 1 litre

3. 1 litre

4. 1 litre

5. 1 litre

6. 1 litre

7. 1 litre

8. 1 litre

9. 1 litre

Write how many litres and millilitres.

10. 1700 ml

10. 1 l 700 ml

11. 2300 ml

12. 1500 ml

13. 3700 ml

14. 2500 ml

15. 4100 ml

16. 1900 ml

17. 2650 ml

18. 1850 ml

Centilitres (cl) and litres (l)

Write how many centilitres of water in each container.

1 1 litre

1. 5 0 cl

2 1 litre

3 1 litre

4 1 litre

5 1 litre

6 1 litre

7 1 litre

8 1 litre

9 1 litre

Write how many centilitres.

10 1 l

10. 1 l = 1 0 0 cl

11 2 l

12 $\frac{1}{2}$ l

13 $1\frac{1}{2}$ l

14 5 l

At Home

Find 10 containers: bottles, cans, cartons, ...
Draw each with its capacity.

Sort them into 2 groups: less than $\frac{1}{2}$ l, more than $\frac{1}{2}$ l.

Millilitres (ml), centilitres (cl) and litres (l)

Write sets of three that contain the same amount.

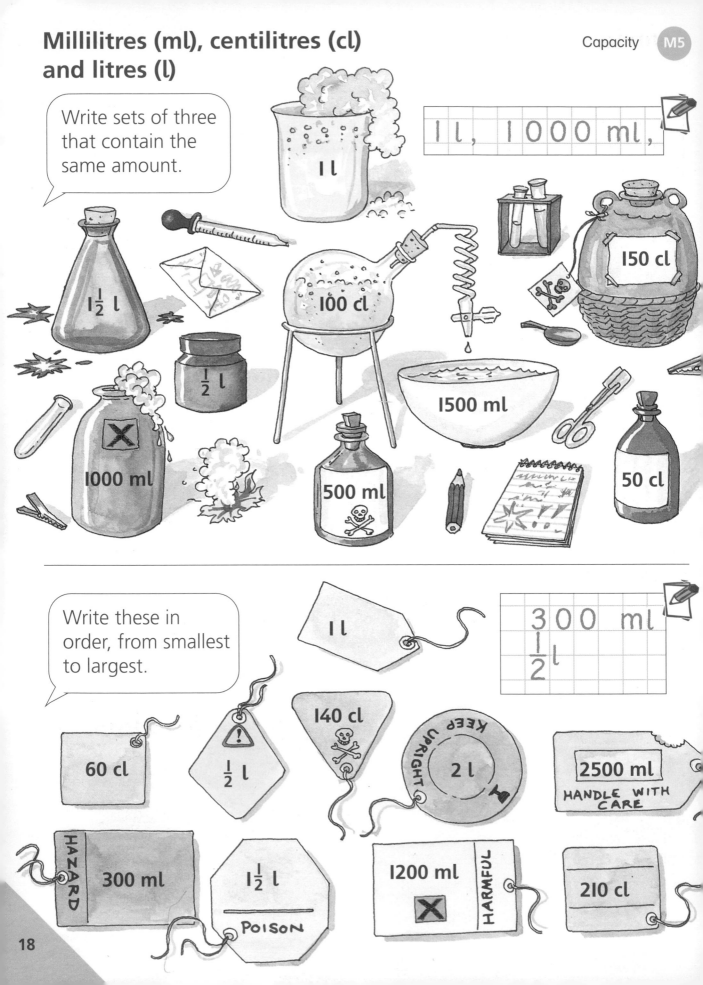

1 l

1 l, 1000 ml,

150 cl

1½ l

100 cl

½ l

1500 ml

1000 ml

500 ml

50 cl

Write these in order, from smallest to largest.

1 l

300 ml
½ l

60 cl

½ l

140 cl

2 l KEEP UPRIGHT

2500 ml
HANDLE WITH CARE

300 ml HAZARD

1½ l POISON

1200 ml HARMFUL

210 cl

Volume

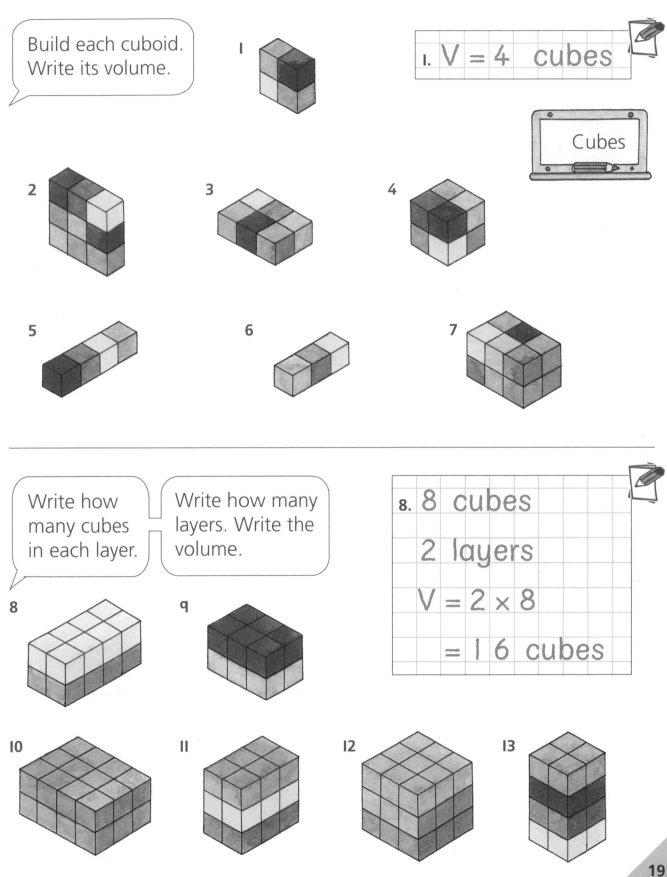

Build each cuboid. Write its volume.

1.

1. V = 4 cubes

Cubes

2

3

4

5

6

7

Write how many cubes in each layer.

Write how many layers. Write the volume.

8. 8 cubes

2 layers

V = 2 × 8

= 16 cubes

8

9

10

11

12

13

Volume

Write the volume of each cuboid.

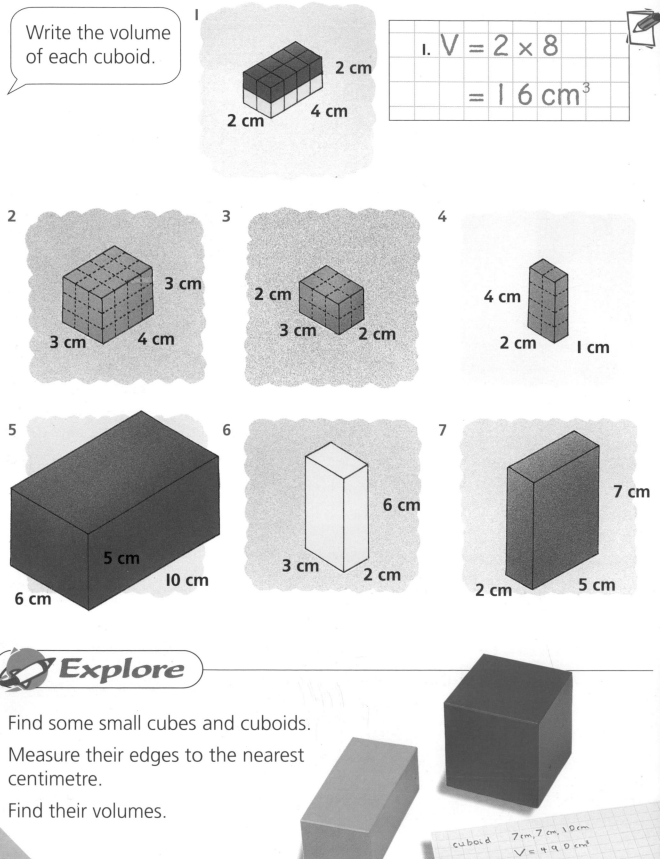

1
2 cm
2 cm
4 cm

1. $V = 2 \times 8$
   $= 16 \, cm^3$

2
3 cm
3 cm
4 cm

3
2 cm
3 cm
2 cm

4
4 cm
2 cm
1 cm

5
5 cm
10 cm
6 cm

6
6 cm
3 cm
2 cm

7
7 cm
2 cm
5 cm

Explore

Find some small cubes and cuboids.

Measure their edges to the nearest centimetre.

Find their volumes.

cuboid 7 cm, 7 cm, 10 cm
$V = 490 \, cm^3$

Telling the time

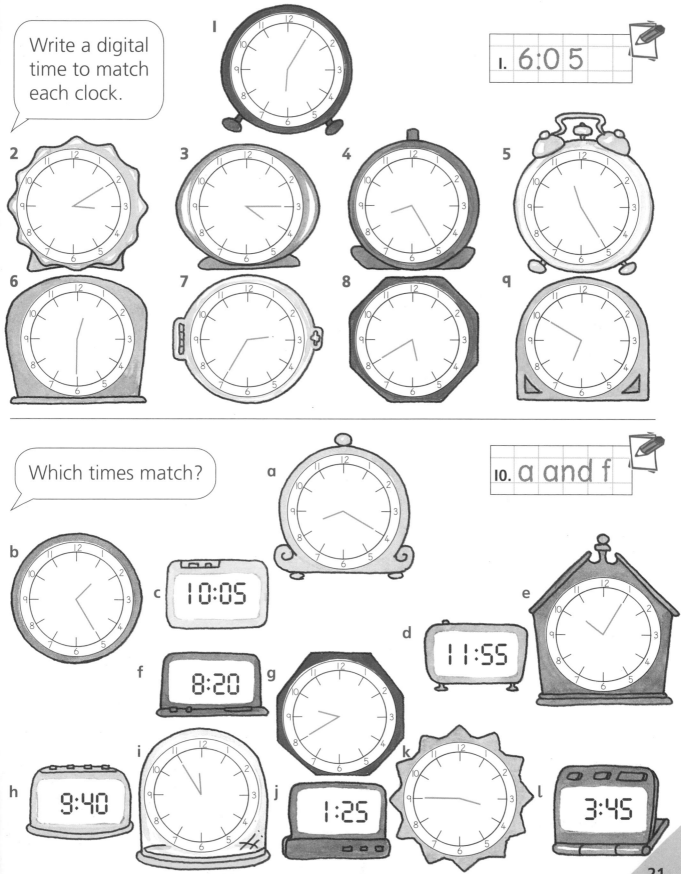

Write a digital time to match each clock.

I. 6:05

Which times match?

10. a and f

Minutes

Write how many minutes past the hour.

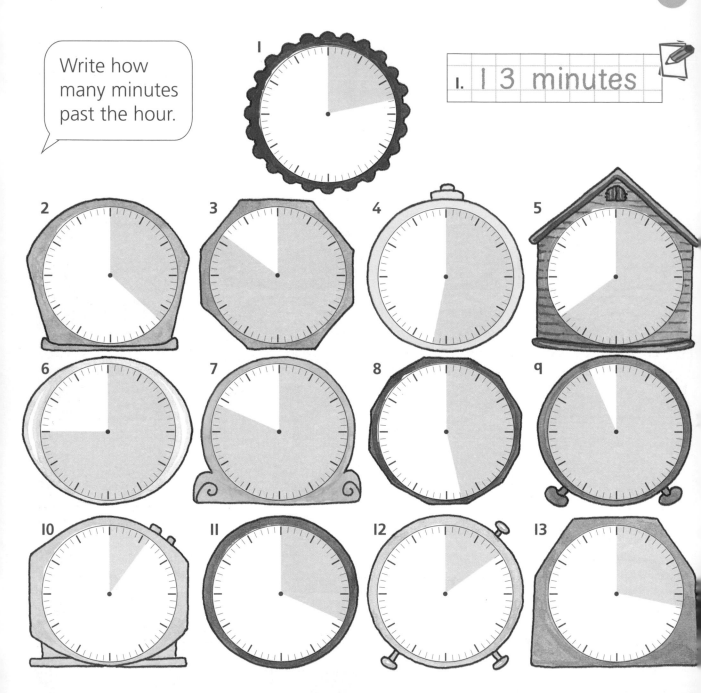

1. 1 3 minutes

For each clock above write how many minutes to the hour.

1. 4 7 minutes

Telling the time

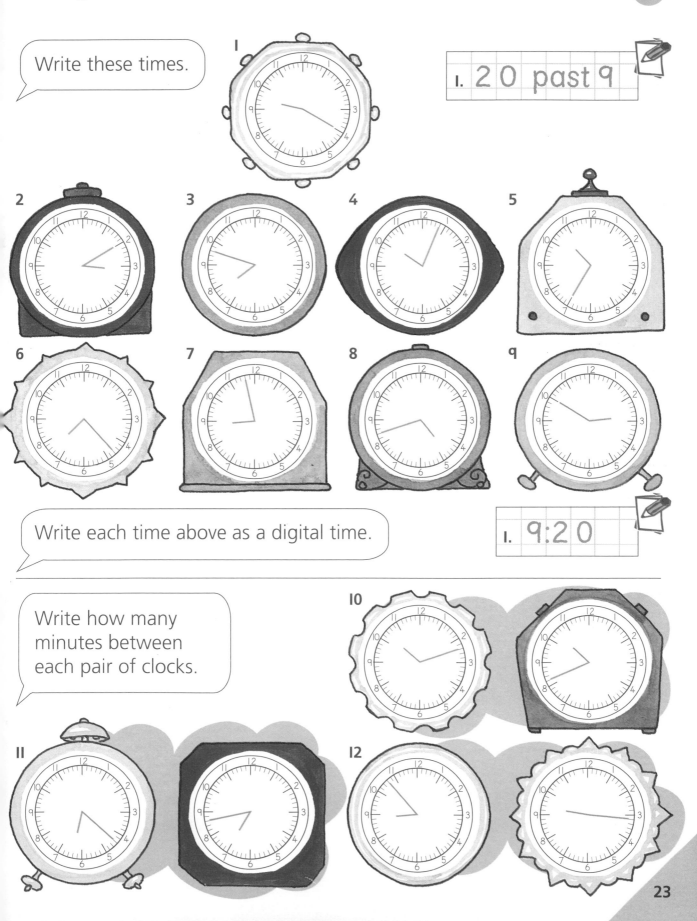

Write these times.

1. 20 past 9

Write each time above as a digital time.

1. 9:20

Write how many minutes between each pair of clocks.

Telling the time

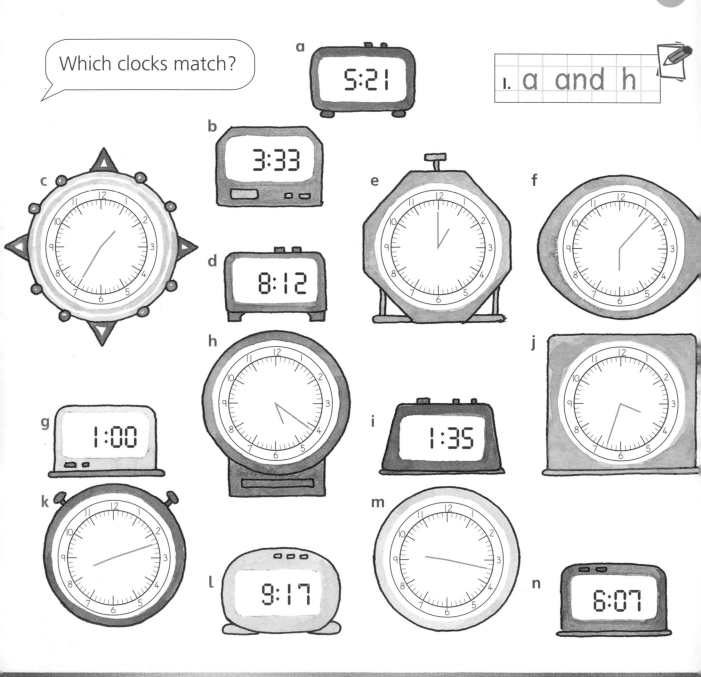

Which clocks match?

a **5:21**

1. a and h

b **3:33**

c

e

f

d **8:12**

h

j

g **1:00**

i **1:35**

k

m

l **9:17**

n **6:07**

At Home

Write a diary, with times, of what you do one day after school.

3:46 → got home
4:02 → played out
5:27 → had tea

Calendars

June

Sun	Mon	Tues	Wed	Thurs	Fri	Sat
1	2 Sam's birthday	3	4	5 Go swimming	6	7
8	9	10	11 Trip to seaside	12	13	14 Amy's party
15 Go to granny's	16	17	18	19 Bike ride	20 Go to cinema	21
22	23 Sports day	24	25	26	27	28 Football game
29	30 Day off school!					

Write the dates of these.

1　Bike ride

1. 19 June

2　Sports day

3　Sam's birthday

4　Amy's party

Write the days these happen.

5　Go swimming

5. Thursday

6　Football game

7　Day off school

8　Go to cinema

How many days after the trip to the seaside is the:

9　Bike ride?

9. 8 days

10　Football game?

11　Day off school?

25

Calendars

			October			
Sun	Mon	Tues	Wed	Thurs	Fri	Sat
				1	2	3
4	5	6	7	8	9	10
11	12	13	14	15	16	17
18	19	20	21	22	23	24
25	26	27	28	29	30	31

Which dates are these?

1   first Monday   1. 5   October

2   second Tuesday   3   first Sunday   4   third Friday

5   first Thursday   6   second Wednesday   7   second Thursday

---

Which date is one week after:

8   14 October?   9   18 October?

10   9 October?   11   5 October?   12   23 October?

Which date is two weeks after:

13   1 October?   14   17 October?

15   10 October?   16   13 October?   17   4 October?

26

Calendars

January
S	M	Tu	W	Th	Fr	Sa
			1	2	3	4
5	6	7	8	9	10	11
12	13	14	15	16	17	18
19	20	21	22	23	24	25
26	27	28	29	30	31	

February
S	M	Tu	W	Th	Fr	Sa
						1
2	3	4	5	6	7	8
9	10	11	12	13	14	15
16	17	18	19	20	21	22
23	24	25	26	27	28	

March
S	M	Tu	W	Th	Fr	Sa
						1
2	3	4	5	6	7	8
9	10	11	12	13	14	15
16	17	18	19	20	21	22
23	24	25	26	27	28	29
30	31					

April
S	M	Tu	W	Th	Fr	Sa
		1	2	3	4	5
6	7	8	9	10	11	12
13	14	15	16	17	18	19
20	21	22	23	24	25	26
27	28	29	30			

May
S	M	Tu	W	Th	Fr	Sa
				1	2	3
4	5	6	7	8	9	10
11	12	13	14	15	16	17
18	19	20	21	22	23	24
25	26	27	28	29	30	31

June
S	M	Tu	W	Th	Fr	Sa
1	2	3	4	5	6	7
8	9	10	11	12	13	14
15	16	17	18	19	20	21
22	23	24	25	26	27	28
29	30					

Write how many:

1 Wednesdays in January

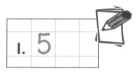

1. 5

2 Tuesdays in February   3 Fridays in April

4 Mondays in March   5 Sundays in June

Which day is the first of: 6 January   6. Wednesday

7 April   8 June   9 May   10 March

Which day is the last of: 11 February   12 June   13 May

14 January   15 April   16 March

How many weekend days are there in each month?

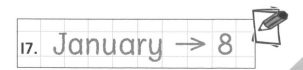

17. January → 8

Timetables

Saturday Programmes on Channel 8	
9:00	Rab and Rob
9:20	Bonzo the dog
9:50	Strange Hill School
10:15	Dragon Quest
10:30	Animal Watch
11:30	Space Cops
12:30	Brainiac Quiz
1:00	News
1:10	Weather

Write the start times of these.

1 Space Cops

1. 11:30

2 Bonzo the dog   3 Animal Watch   4 Rab and Rob

5 Brainiac Quiz   6 News   7 Dragon Quest

Write the end time for each.

1. 12:30

Which programmes start at these times?

8. News

28

Winston and Annie have planned their Saturday.

Our Saturday		
8:00	Breakfast	
8:20	Dress and wash	
9:05	Watch TV	
9:30	Play in garden	
9:55	Go to park	
12:00	Lunch	
12:30	Wash up	
12:45	Tidy room and change	
2:00	Jo's party	
5:10	Go home	

How much time do they spend:

1 having breakfast?

1. 20 minutes

2 in the garden?

3 at Jo's party?

4 having lunch?

How much time between:

5 breakfast and lunch?

6 Jo's party and going home?

7 lunch and Jo's party?

8 watching TV and lunch?

9 breakfast and watching TV?

Write your own timetable for next Saturday.

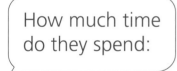

My Saturday
8:30 → get up, get dressed

Timetables

How long does it take from the bus station to:

	Blue 3a	
	Bus Station	8:50
	Church	8:57
	School	9:08
	Clock Tower	9:13
	Shops	9:20
	Post Office	9:26
	Hospital	9:41
	Telephone Box	9:53
	Pond	10:00
	Bus Station	10:12

1. 1. 7 minutes

2.

3.

4.

How long does it take from:

5. church to school

6. clock tower to shops

7. post office to pond

8. bus station to school

9. school to hospital

10. church to telephone

11. clock tower to pond

12. post office to bus station

Explore

Find the length of time between each stop on the timetable. Write them in order.

Which is the longest?
Which is the shortest?

bus station → church 7 minutes
church → school 11 minutes
school → clock tower

Seconds

How many seconds have passed?

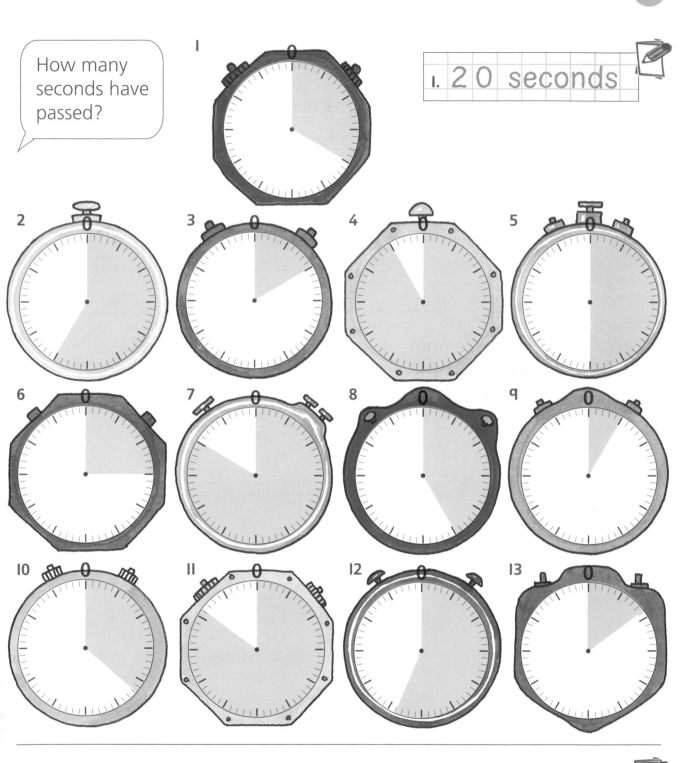

1. 2 0 seconds

For each stopwatch above write how many seconds to the next minute.

1. 4 0 seconds

Write how many minutes and seconds.

1. I minute 2 5 seconds

I	85 seconds	2	96 seconds	3	100 seconds
4	110 seconds	5	120 seconds	6	145 seconds
7	82 seconds	8	130 seconds	9	102 seconds

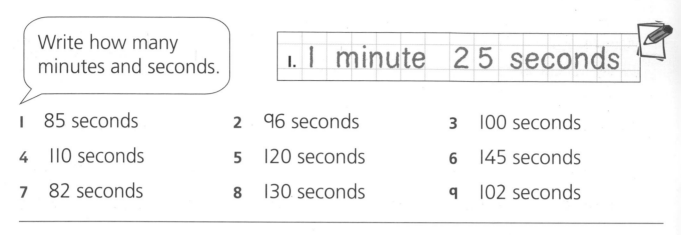

Runner	Jo	Phil	Uma	Ros	John	Sam	June	Anup	Tom	Raj
Time (s)	95	112	151	132	170	85	142	81	185	99

Which children finished in:

10 under $1\frac{1}{2}$ minutes?

10. Sam, Anup

11 between $1\frac{1}{2}$ and 2 minutes?

12 between 2 and $2\frac{1}{2}$ minutes?

13 between $2\frac{1}{2}$ and 3 minutes?

14 over 3 minutes?

Who finished:

15 first?

16 third?

17 last?

Seconds

> Write how many seconds.

1   I minute 20 seconds

1. 8 0 seconds

2   I minute I0 seconds

3   I minute 30 seconds

4   I minute 45 seconds

5   I minute I5 seconds

6   I minute 5 seconds

7   2 minutes 5 seconds

8   2 minutes 25 seconds

9   I minute 35 seconds

10   2 minutes 35 seconds

> Every 10 seconds you score one point.

> Write how many points in total.

11   40 seconds

11. 4 0 seconds

4 points

12   I minute 10 seconds

13   I minute 30 seconds

14   2 minutes

15   2 minutes 10 seconds

16   3 minutes

17   I minute 20 seconds

Explore

Use a calculator.

Find how many seconds in:
5 minutes, half an hour, an hour.

Find how many seconds in other lengths of time.

5 minutes
= 5 × 60
= 3 0 0 seconds

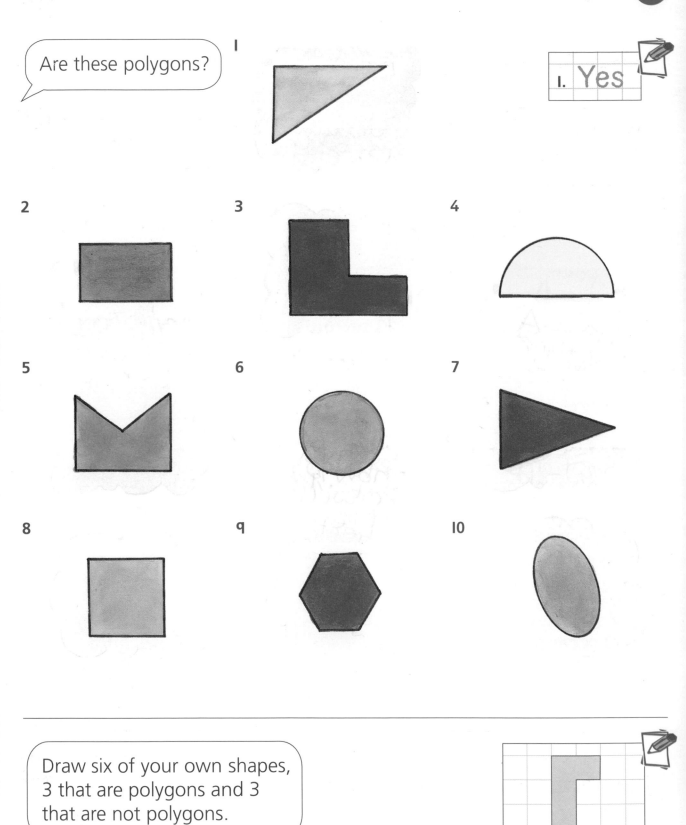

Are these polygons?

1

1. Yes

2

3

4

5

6

7

8

9

10

Draw six of your own shapes, 3 that are polygons and 3 that are not polygons.

polygon

Naming shapes

triangle   rectangle   pentagon   hexagon   octagon

Write the name of each shape.

1.

I. rectangle

2.

3.

4.

5.

6.

7.

8.

9.

10.

Draw these shapes.

11 pentagon

12 square

13 triangle

14 hexagon

15 rectangle

16 octagon

II.

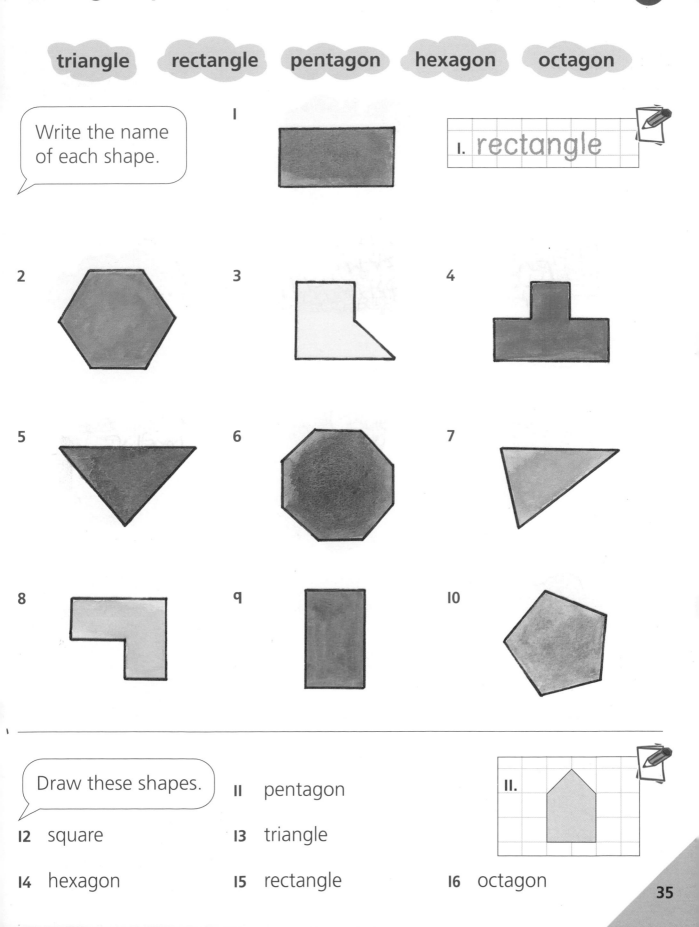

Naming shapes

Write how many sides and the name.

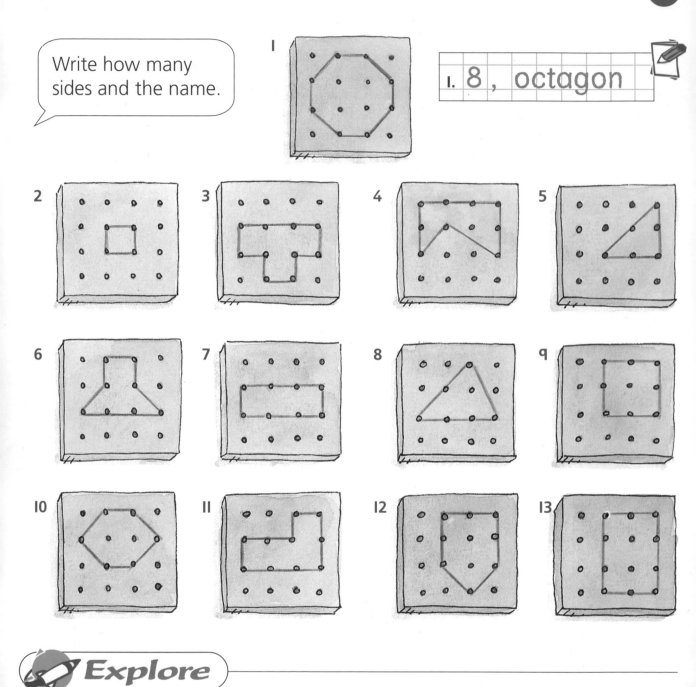

1. 8 , octagon

Explore

Use a 3x3 geoboard (or spotty paper).

Make a polygon with 3 sides.
Make polygons with different numbers of sides. Record each.

What is the largest number of sides you can make?

Circles

Measure the radius of each circle.

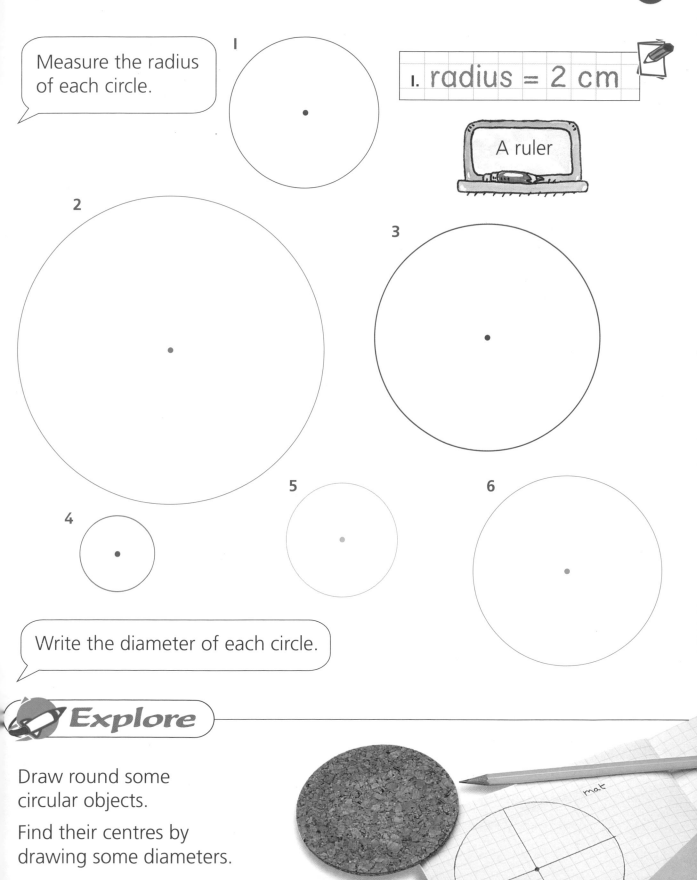

1. radius = 2 cm

A ruler

Write the diameter of each circle.

Explore

Draw round some circular objects.

Find their centres by drawing some diameters.

Measure the diameter of each circle.

1.

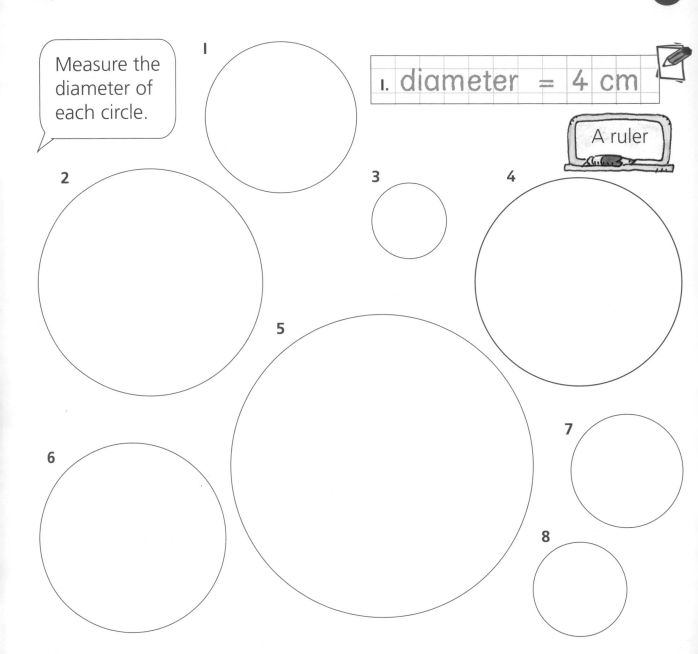

1. diameter = 4 cm

A ruler

Nets

Write which shapes are in each net.

1

I. 4 rectangles,
2 squares

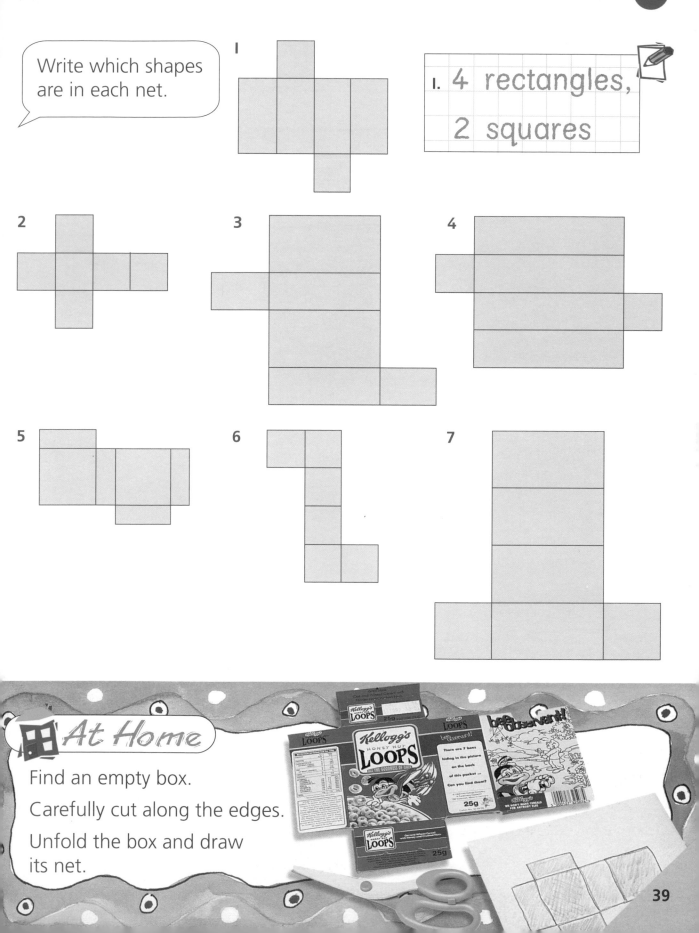

2

3

4

5

6

7

At Home

Find an empty box.

Carefully cut along the edges.

Unfold the box and draw its net.

39

Nets

Are these shapes the nets of cubes?

I

I. Yes

2

3

4

5

6

7

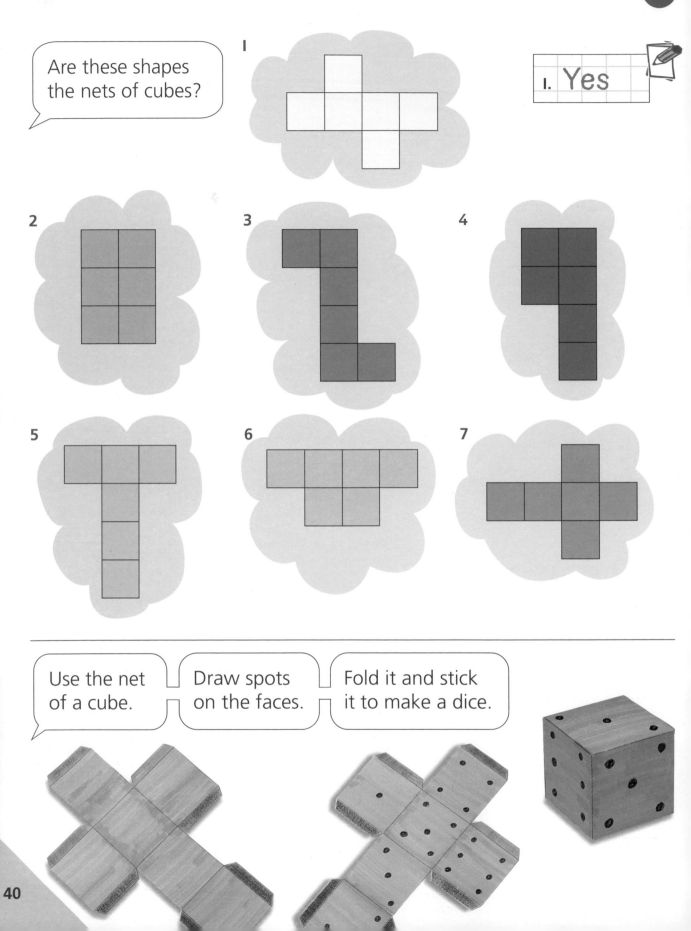

Use the net of a cube.

Draw spots on the faces.

Fold it and stick it to make a dice.

Pyramids and cones

For each shape write pyramid or cone.

1. pyramid

1

2

3

4

5

6

Write the shape of each base.

1. triangle

Write the name of each shape.

1. triangle-based pyramid

For each shape write how many faces, edges and vertices.

1. 4 faces

   6 edges

   4 vertices

Naming shapes

cone pyramid sphere prism cuboid cube cylinder

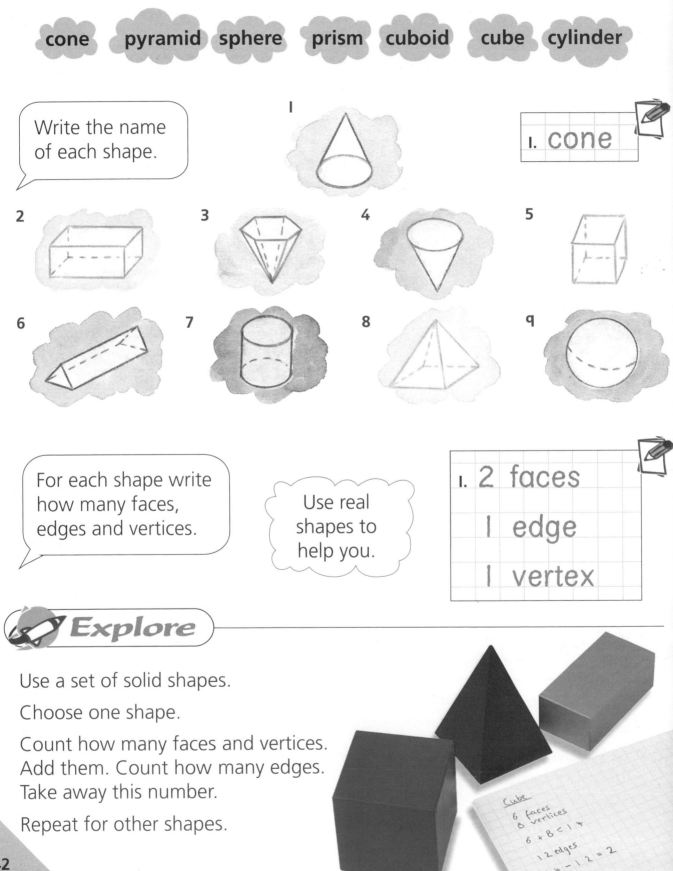

Write the name of each shape.

I.

1. cone

2

3

4

5

6

7

8

9

For each shape write how many faces, edges and vertices.

Use real shapes to help you.

1. 2 faces
   1 edge
   1 vertex

Explore

Use a set of solid shapes.

Choose one shape.

Count how many faces and vertices. Add them. Count how many edges. Take away this number.

Repeat for other shapes.

Cube
6 faces
8 vertices
6 + 8 < 14
12 edges
14 − 12 = 2

42

Half-turns

One shape from each pair has been rotated a half-turn.

Write the pairs.

1. A and H

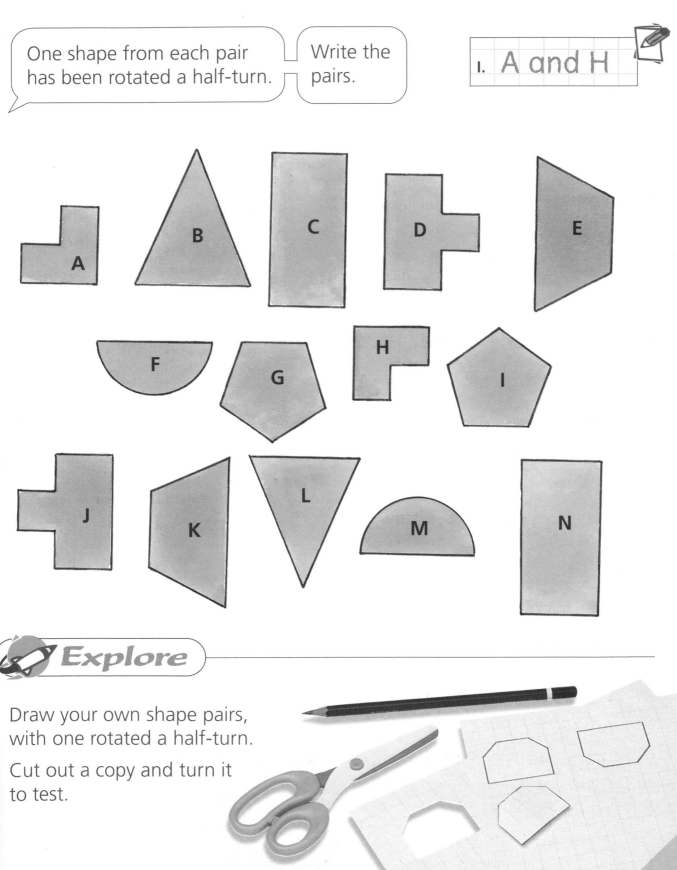

Explore

Draw your own shape pairs, with one rotated a half-turn.

Cut out a copy and turn it to test.

Draw the position of each shape after each of 4 quarter-turns.

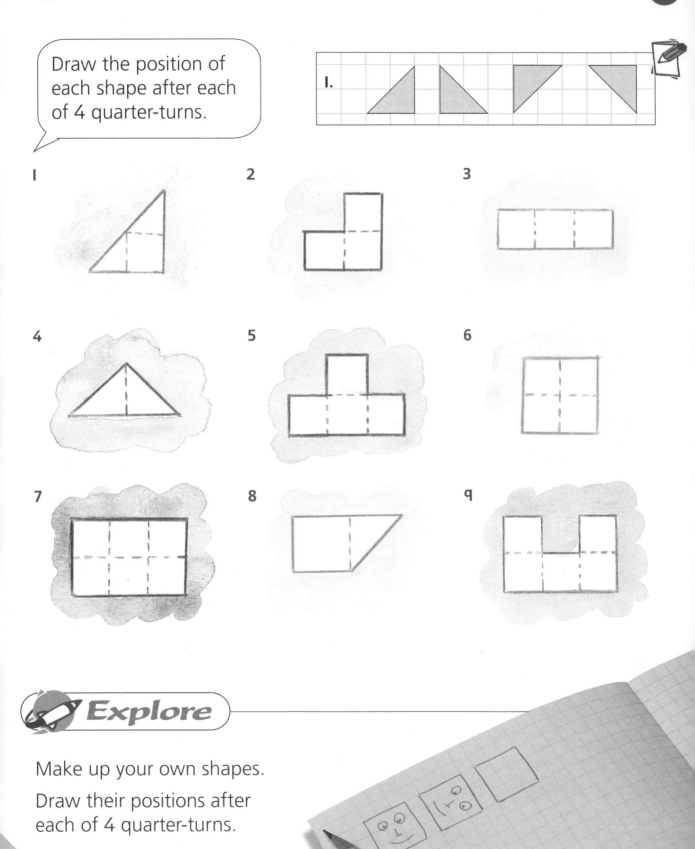

I.

1

2

3

4

5

6

7

8

9

![Explore]

Make up your own shapes.

Draw their positions after each of 4 quarter-turns.

Compass points

Write the direction each fish is facing.

1

1. east

2

3

4

N

5

6

7

8

9

10

11

12

Write the direction each fish faces after one half-turn.

1

1. west

Explore

North and south are **opposite** directions.

Write some other pairs of opposite directions.

N

S

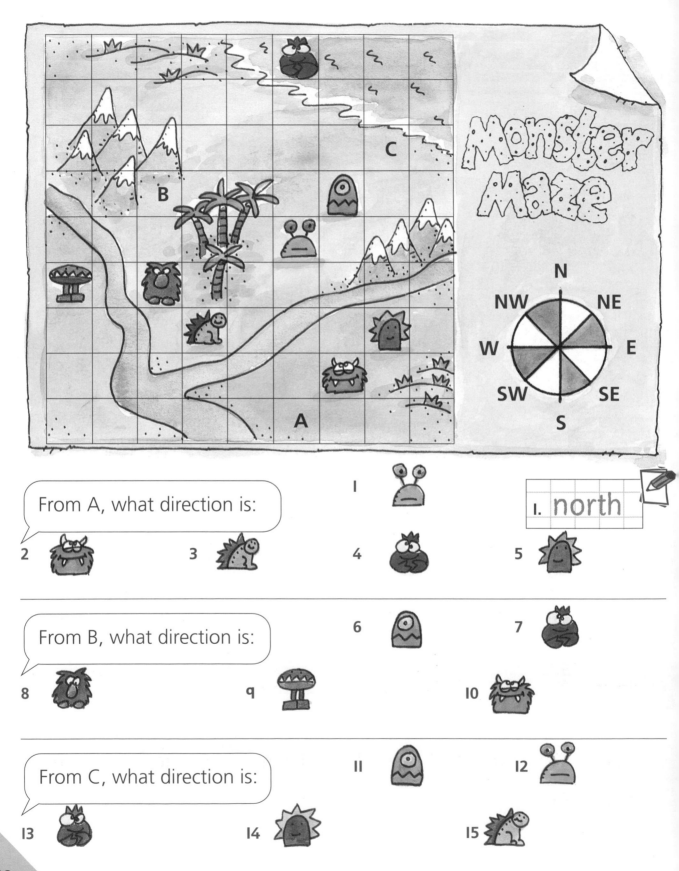

From A, what direction is:

1. north

2   3   4   5

From B, what direction is:

6   7

8   9   10

From C, what direction is:

11   12

13   14   15

Compass points

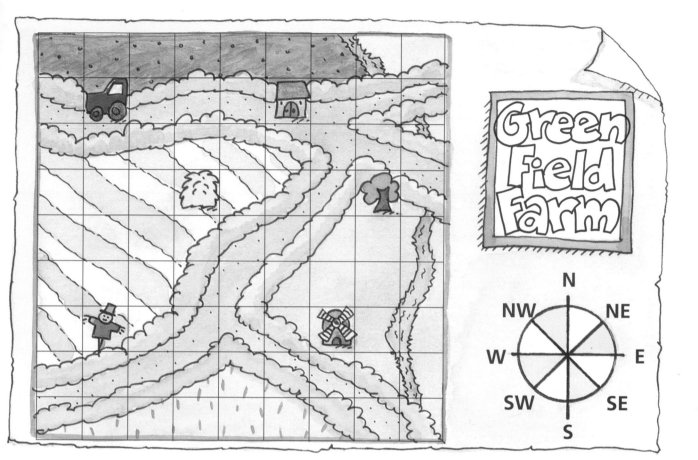

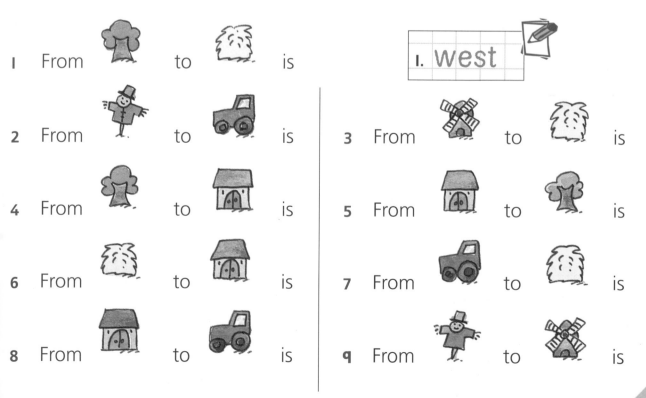

1 From 🌳 to 🌾 is

2 From 🎃 to 🚜 is

3 From 🏭 to 🌾 is

4 From 🌳 to 🏠 is

5 From 🏠 to 🌳 is

6 From 🌾 to 🏠 is

7 From 🚜 to 🌾 is

8 From 🏠 to 🚜 is

9 From 🎃 to 🏭 is

47

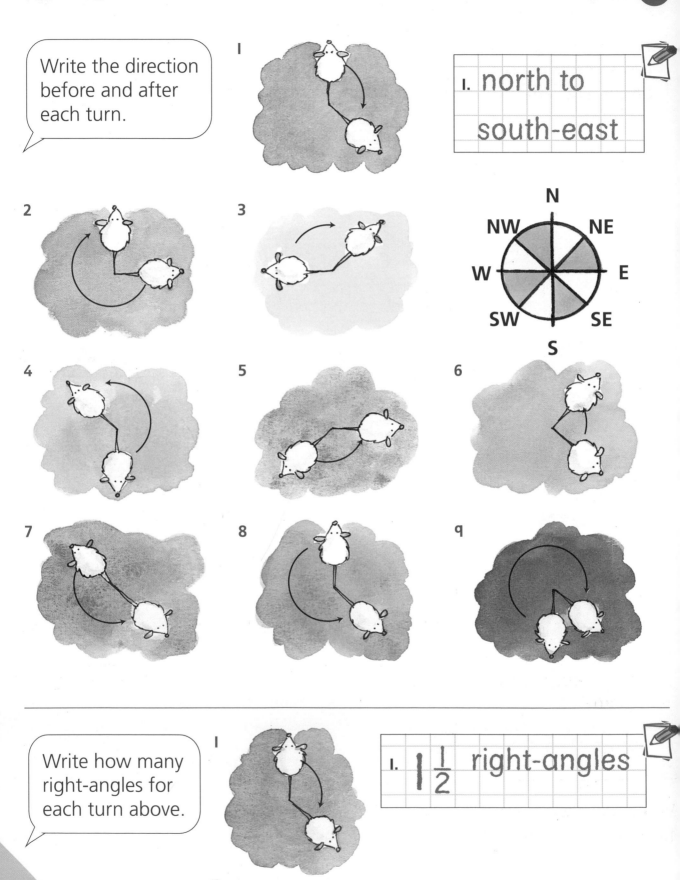

Write the direction before and after each turn.

1. north to south-east

2

3

4

5

6

7

8

9

Compass:
N
NW   NE
W   E
SW   SE
S

Write how many right-angles for each turn above.

1. $1\frac{1}{2}$ right-angles

Turning

Write the direction before and after each turn.

I

2 right-angles

I. north to south

2

I right-angle

3

2 right-angles

4

I½ right-angles

5

2½ right-angles

6

½ right-angle

7

3 right-angles

8

I right-angle

9

½ right-angle

10

3½ right-angles

Write clockwise or anticlockwise for each turn above.

I. anticlockwise

Explore

Write 4 different turns that finish facing south-east.

face north
turn clockwise
1½ right angles

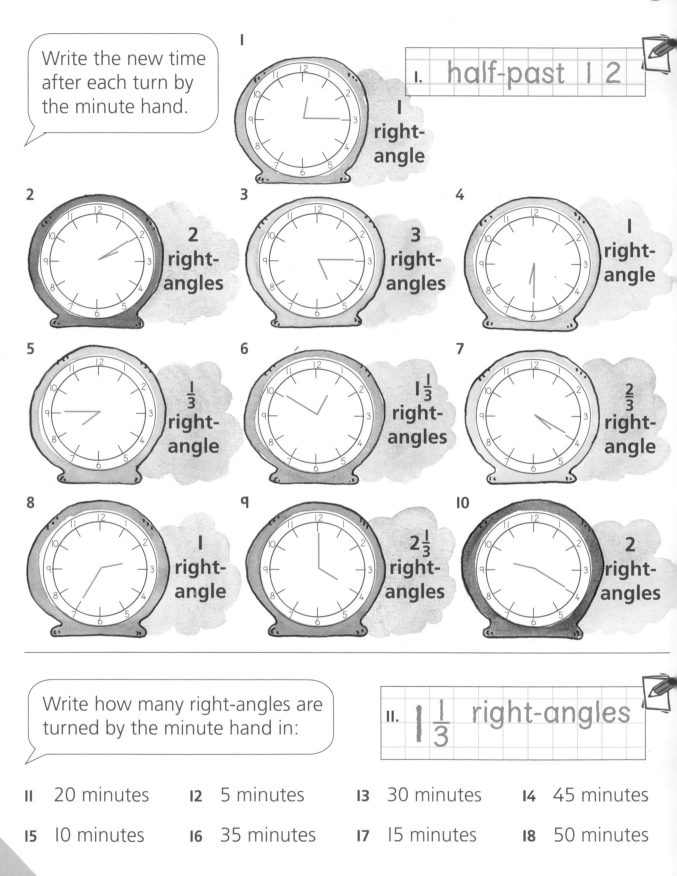

Write the new time after each turn by the minute hand.

I.   I   1 right-angle   I. **half-past 12**

2   2 right-angles

3   3 right-angles

4   1 right-angle

5   $\frac{1}{3}$ right-angle

6   $1\frac{1}{3}$ right-angles

7   $\frac{2}{3}$ right-angle

8   1 right-angle

9   $2\frac{1}{3}$ right-angles

10   2 right-angles

Write how many right-angles are turned by the minute hand in:

II. $1\frac{1}{3}$ **right-angles**

II   20 minutes   I2   5 minutes   I3   30 minutes   I4   45 minutes

I5   I0 minutes   I6   35 minutes   I7   I5 minutes   I8   50 minutes

Coordinates

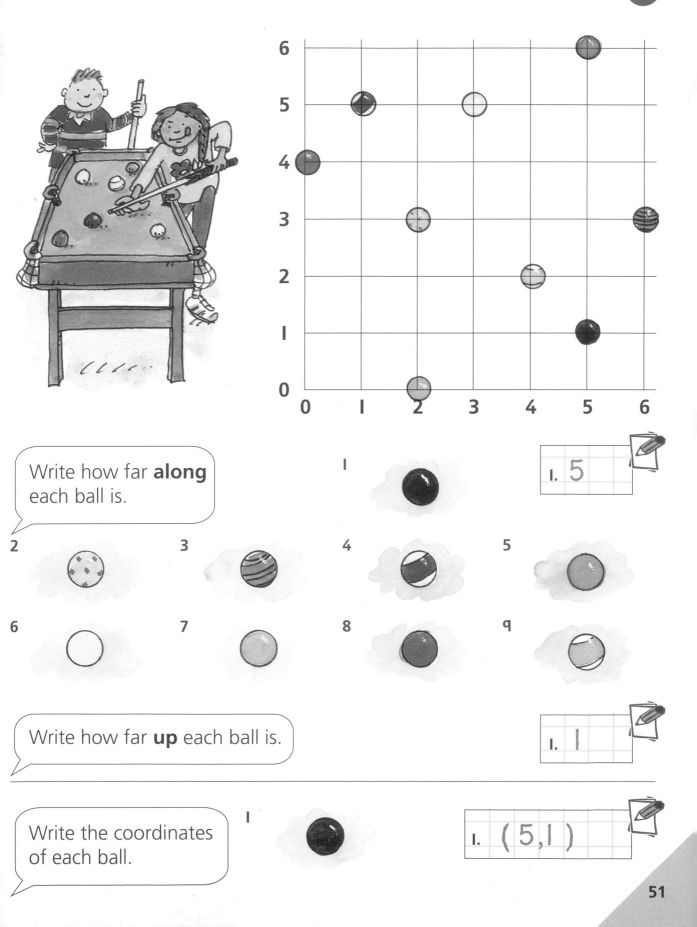

Write how far **along** each ball is.

1. 5

1

2

3

4

5

6

7

8

9

Write how far **up** each ball is.

1. 1

Write the coordinates of each ball.

1

1. (5,1)

Coordinates

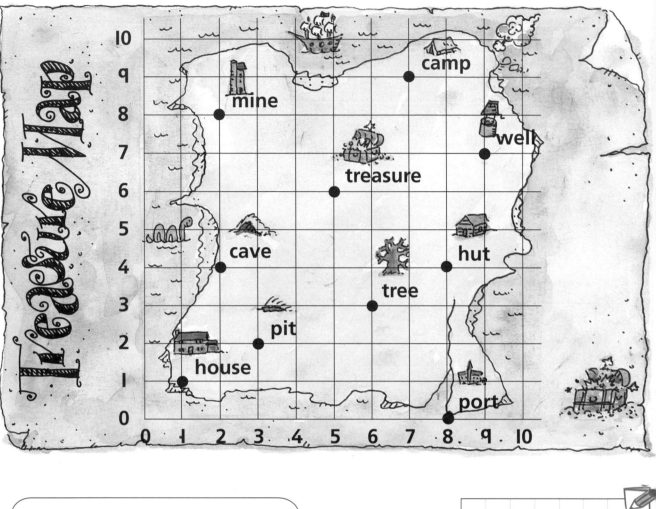

Write the coordinates of these.

1. (2,4)

1	cave	2	treasure	3	hut	4	pit	5	mine

1 cave   2 treasure   3 hut   4 pit   5 mine

6 camp   7 house   8 port   9 tree   10 well

Explore

Draw your own grid and map on squared paper.

Mark some places where the lines cross.

Write their coordinates.

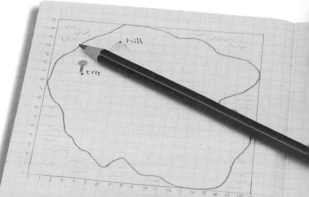

52

Coordinates

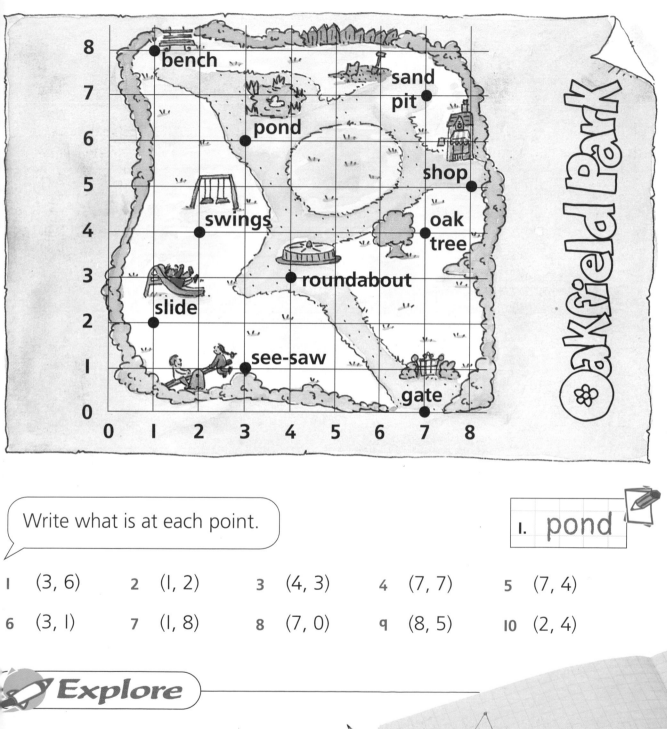

> Write what is at each point.

| 1. pond |

1 (3, 6)   2 (1, 2)   3 (4, 3)   4 (7, 7)   5 (7, 4)

6 (3, 1)   7 (1, 8)   8 (7, 0)   9 (8, 5)   10 (2, 4)

Explore

Draw your own grid on squared paper.

Draw a straight-line shape.

Write the coordinates of
its corners.

53

Our favourite TV Programmes

Programme	Total votes
Space Cops	45
House of fun	22
Dragon Quest	32
Stumpy and pod	15
Redland Road	30
Robodog	20
Pop charts	25

Which programmes had these votes?

1 20

ı. Robodog

2 22   3 32   4 most   5 second most   6 fewes

How many voted for: 7 Space Cops   8 Pop Charts   ɋ Redland Road

10 Space Cops **or** Dragon Quest   ıı Redland Road **or** Robodog

At Home

Find some knives, forks, spoons, …

Count how many of each and draw a frequency table.

Our cutlery	
Type	Number
knives	8
forks	

Tables

Count how many times each vowel appears in this rhyme.

Vowels are the letters a, e, i, o, u.

As I was going up the stair,
I met a man who wasn't there.
He wasn't there again today,
Oh! How I wish he'd go away.

Copy and complete the table.

vowel	total
a	
e	
i	
o	
u	

Which vowel appeared:

1 7 times?

1. i

2 12 times? **3** 6 times? **4** most? **5** least? **6** second most?

Which of these appeared most often?

7. e, 1 more

7 e **or** i **8** i **or** o **9** o **or** u

10 u **or** a **11** a **or** e **12** e **or** u

Explore

Find a short piece of writing.

Count how many times each vowel appears.

Complete a table and write about the results.

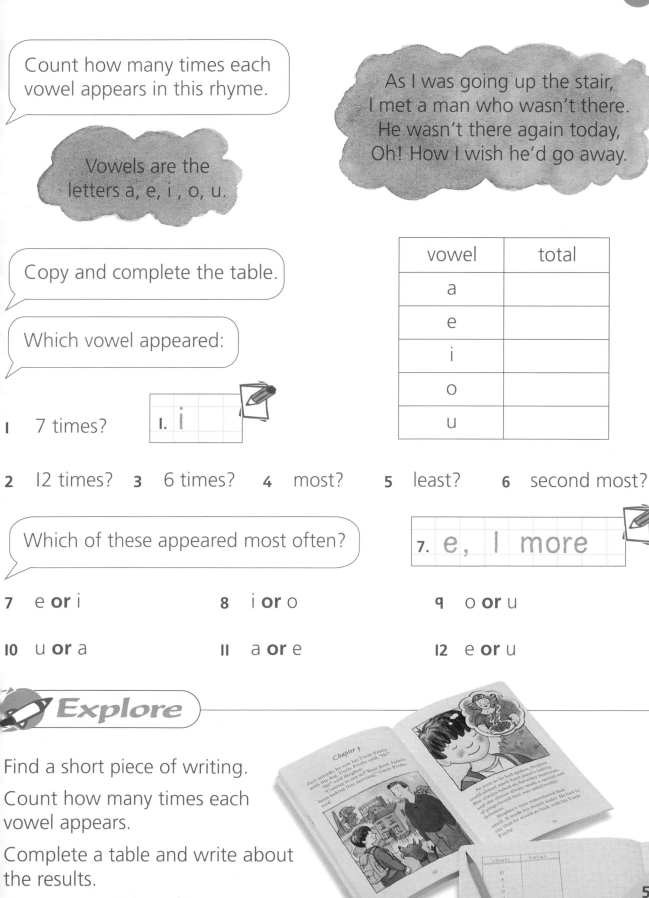

Bar graphs

Our pets

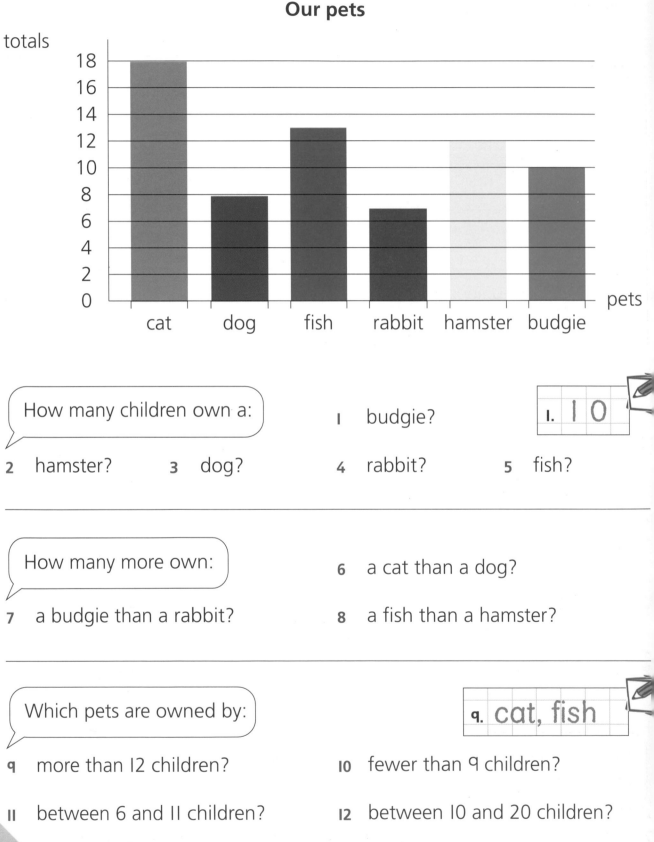

totals

pets

How many children own a:

1 budgie?

2 hamster?   3 dog?   4 rabbit?   5 fish?

1. | 0

How many more own:

6 a cat than a dog?

7 a budgie than a rabbit?   8 a fish than a hamster?

Which pets are owned by:

9 more than 12 children?   10 fewer than 9 children?

11 between 6 and 11 children?   12 between 10 and 20 children?

9. cat, fish

Bar graphs

How we come to school

Number	Transport
20	Car
7	Bike
12	Foot
5	Coach
9	Bus
2	Roller-blades
4	Other

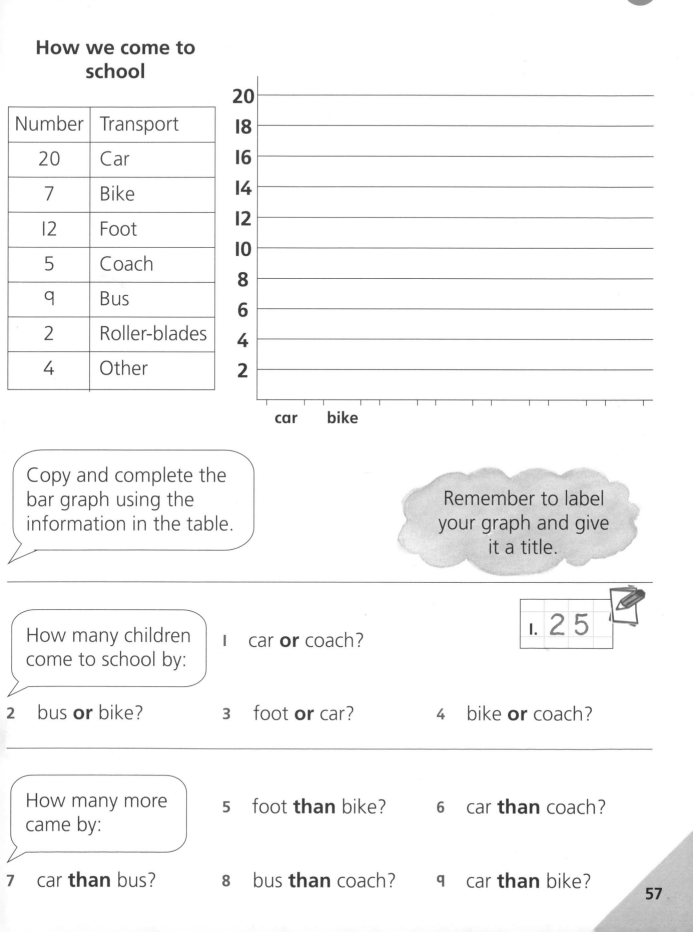

> Copy and complete the bar graph using the information in the table.

> Remember to label your graph and give it a title.

> How many children come to school by:

1 car **or** coach?

1. 2 5

2 bus **or** bike?

3 foot **or** car?

4 bike **or** coach?

> How many more came by:

5 foot **than** bike?

6 car **than** coach?

7 car **than** bus?

8 bus **than** coach?

9 car **than** bike?

Databases

Baseball results

Team		Games won	Games lost	Games drawn
	Tigers	7	2	1
	Eagles	2	6	2
	Rockets	3	2	5
	Sharks	3	3	4
	Jets	2	6	2
	Pirates	4	2	4

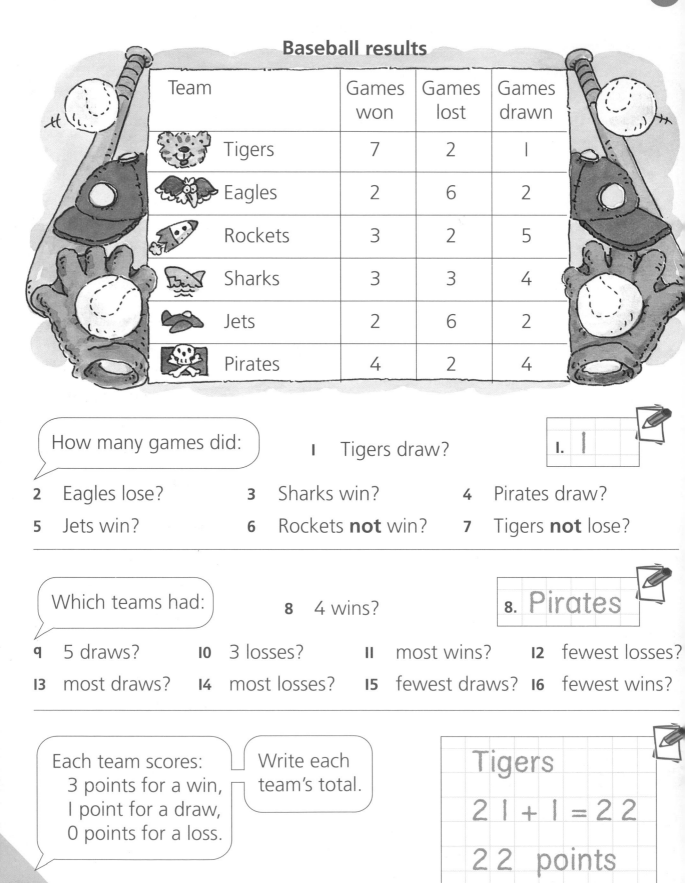

How many games did:

1　Tigers draw?

1. 1

2　Eagles lose?　　3　Sharks win?　　4　Pirates draw?

5　Jets win?　　6　Rockets **not** win?　　7　Tigers **not** lose?

Which teams had:

8　4 wins?

8. Pirates

9　5 draws?　　10　3 losses?　　11　most wins?　　12　fewest losses?

13　most draws?　　14　most losses?　　15　fewest draws?　　16　fewest wins?

Each team scores:
3 points for a win,
1 point for a draw,
0 points for a loss.

Write each team's total.

Tigers

21 + 1 = 22

22 points

Databases

Superhero addresses

Superhero	House Number	Road	Town	Telephone Number
Spider girl	8	Feet Lane	Web Town	60123
Dino-man	3	Cave Close	Rexville	4865
Jet woman	10	Rocket Road	Presto	10651
Robodog	4	Kennel Avenue	Canine	
Supersnake	1	Scale Road	Hisslip	2842
Powerboy	85	Cell Lane	Watt City	29317
The Wasp	6	Nest Street	Hive Town	98765

Who lives in:

1 Cave Close?

1. **Dino-man**

2 Hisslip?   3 Cell Lane?   4 Presto?   5 Feet Lane?

Who has:

6 no phone number?

8. **Robodog**

7 an odd house number?   8 a 4-digit phone number?

9 a 2-digit house number?   10 an even phone number?

What is:

11 Supersnake's house number?   12 Jet woman's home town

13 The Wasp's phone number?   14 Powerboy's home town?

Explore

Choose 5 friends.

Make up some questions to ask them, and draw a database.

My friends

Name	Eye colour	Hair colour	Age
Jo	blue		

Copy and complete this database.

Number	Door colour	Wall colour	House/ Bungalow	Number of front windows
13	green			

At Home

Choose 8 homes near you.

Draw your own database.

Likely and unlikely

Impossible   Unlikely   Likely   Certain

Write one label for each event.

1. Unlikely

1 It will snow tomorrow.

2 I will use a computer today.

3 I will be famous one day.

4 I will fly next week.

5 I will see a dragon tomorrow.

6 I will be older next year.

7 I will sleep next week.

8 I will read a book next week.

9 I will eat tomorrow.

10 I will go to Mars one day.

11 It will be dark tonight.

12 I will play football this week.

13 I will be rich one day.

14 I will eat cheese this week.

15 I will watch TV tonight.

16 I will drive a car one day.

Write 2 impossible and 2 certain events.

Draw a picture for each.

My dog will speak tomorrow – impossible

hello!

Likely and unlikely

Impossible
I will see sheep fly tonight.

Unlikely
There will be a full moon tonight.

Likely
I will watch TV tonight.

Certain
I will sleep tonight.

Write your own 4 events for tomorrow.

Write your own 4 events for next week.

Explore

Work with a partner.

Write each of your 'unlikely' and 'likely' events from above on a card.

Place the cards in a long line from least likely to most likely.

Agree with your partner where each card should go.

I will eat tomorrow.

It will snow tomorrow.

I will read a bo... next week.

Equal chances

Here are 30 dice throws.

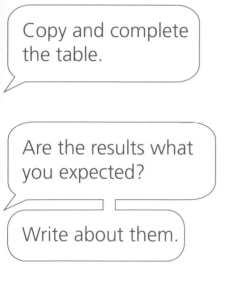

Copy and complete the table.

Are the results what you expected?

Write about them.

Dice throw	Tallies	Totals
1		
2		
3		
4		
5		
6		

Explore

Work with a partner.

Throw a dice 30 times.

Draw and complete a table.

Write about the results.

Equal chances

Here are 24 dice throws.

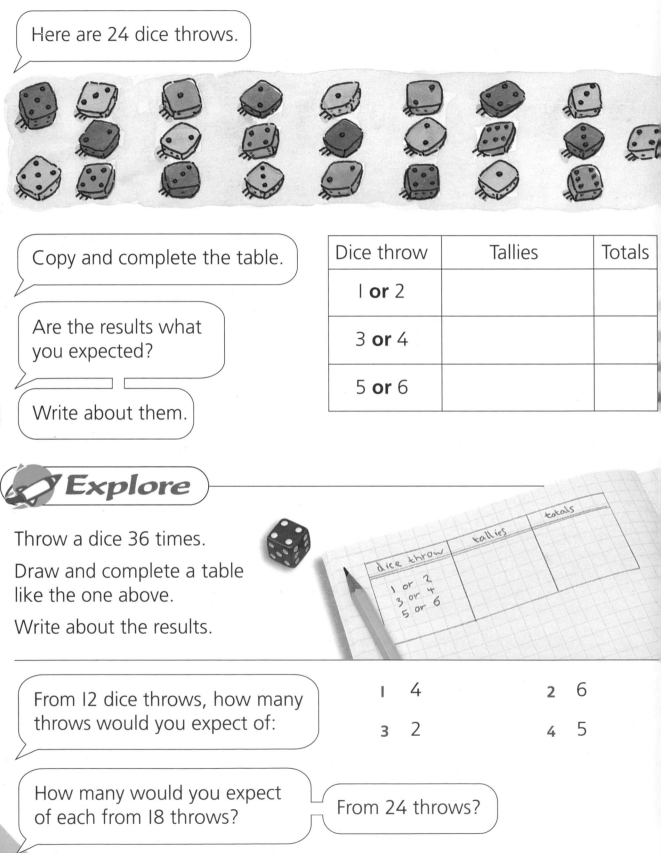

Copy and complete the table.

Are the results what you expected?

Write about them.

Dice throw	Tallies	Totals
1 **or** 2		
3 **or** 4		
5 **or** 6		

Explore

Throw a dice 36 times.

Draw and complete a table like the one above.

Write about the results.

From 12 dice throws, how many throws would you expect of:

1	4	2	6
3	2	4	5

How many would you expect of each from 18 throws?

From 24 throws?